Other FoxTrot Books by Bill Amend

FoxTrot
Pass the Loot
Black Bart Says Draw
Eight Yards, Down and Out
Bury My Heart at Fun-Fun Mountain
Say Hello to Cactus Flats
May the Force Be With Us, Please
Take Us to Your Mall
The Return of the Lone Iguana
At Least This Place Sells T-Shirts
Come Closer, Roger, There's a Mosquito on Your Nose
Welcome to Jasorassic Park

Anthologies

FoxTrot: The Works
FoxTrot *en masse*
Enormously FoxTrot
Wildly FoxTrot
FoxTrot Beyond a Doubt

CAMP FOXTROT

by Bill Amend

**Andrews McMeel
Publishing**

Kansas City

FoxTrot is distributed internationally by Universal Press Syndicate.

Camp FoxTrot copyright © 1998 by Bill Amend. All rights reserved. Printed in the United States of America. No part of this book may be used or reproduced in any manner whatsoever without written permission except in the case of reprints in the context of reviews. For information, write Andrews McMeel Publishing, 4520 Main Street, Kansas City, Missouri 64111.

Information about Andrews McMeel Publishing can be found at www.andrewsmcmeel.com

98 99 00 01 02 BAM 10 9 8 7 6 5 4 3 2

ISBN: 0-8362-6747-8

Library of Congress Catalog Card Number: 98-85335

Visit *FoxTrot* on the World Wide Web at www.foxtrot.com

YOU BROUGHT **MORE** OFFICE WORK HOME?! | IT'S NOT MY FAULT! I SWEAR!

PEMBROOK KEEPS GIVING ME THESE BIG ASSIGNMENTS THE NIGHT BEFORE THEY'RE DUE.

IT'S ALMOST AS IF HE **WANTS** ME TO TAKE THIS STUFF HOME.

I JUST DON'T GET IT. | OH, I'M SURE HE'S GOT **SOME** WEIRD REASON.

DAD, I FOUND ANOTHER MATH MISTAKE.

JUST WHO DOES MY TEACHER THINK SHE IS?!

SERIOUSLY! SHE'S A SADIST! MY WHOLE WEEKEND IS RUINED BECAUSE OF HER!

I HAVE A GOOD MIND TO REPORT HER TO THE SCHOOL BOARD! WHERE'S THE PHONE BOOK?!

YOU KNOW, JASON, SOME OF US WOULD GIVE A KIDNEY FOR A WEEKEND WITHOUT HOMEWORK. | I SUPPOSE I COULD GET A JUMP ON MY SUMMER READING LIST...

...AND THEN ONCE I BECOME RICH AND SUCCESSFUL, I'LL PROBABLY BUY A DODGE VIPER.

ACTUALLY, WHAT I WANT TO DO IS GET **TWO** VIPERS— A RED ONE FOR DAYTIME DRIVING AND A STEALTHY BLACK ONE FOR NIGHT.

IN FACT, I OUGHTA JUST GET ONE IN EVERY COLOR THEY MAKE. IT'S NOT LIKE MY MANSION WON'T HAVE ENOUGH GARAGE SPACE.

PETER, HAVE YOU EVEN **STARTED** YOUR HOMEWORK?! | MOM, C'MON— I'M PLANNING FOR MY FUTURE!

ALL I WANT IS A SPACE SHUTTLE.

FoxTrot
BILL AMEND

FoxTrot
BILL AMEND

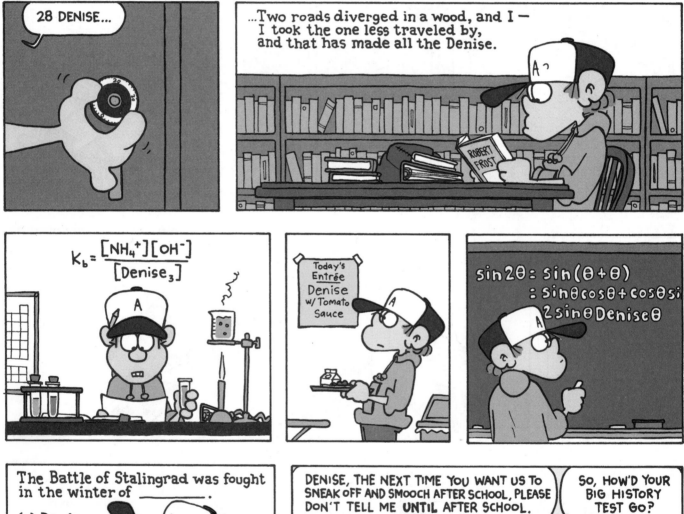

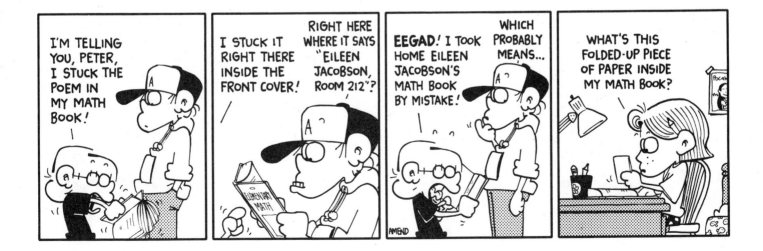

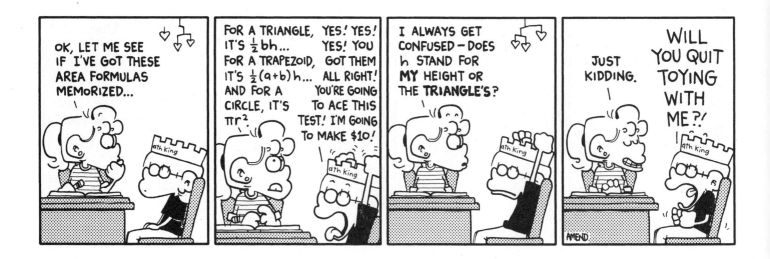

18

FoxTrot
BILL AMEND

FoxTrot
BILL AMEND

A Tale of Two Cities
By Charles Dickens

As Read By David Copperfield

" It was the best of times, it was the worst of times "...

CLOTHES + STUFF

"Madame Defarge, his wife, sat in the shop behind the counter as he came in."...

" 'Oh! they'll find him guilty,' said the other. 'Don't you be afraid of that.' "...

" 'Dear Doctor Manette, I love your daughter fondly, dearly, disinterestedly, devotedly.' "...

"During all that time Lucie was never s— f G Z P hour to hour, but th—t the Guillot;

BONK! BONK!

MISSION IMPOSSI II: THE COMIC STRIP DEADLINE COMING SO

AMEND

HOW AM I SUPPOSED TO GET MY SUMMER READING DONE WITH A WALKMAN THAT KEEPS BREAKING?!

PERMIT ME TO COUNT TO 10 BEFORE ANSWERING.

WHAT I WISH THEY'D MAKE ARE CLIFFS NOTES BOOKS ON TAPE.

FoxTrot
BILL AMEND

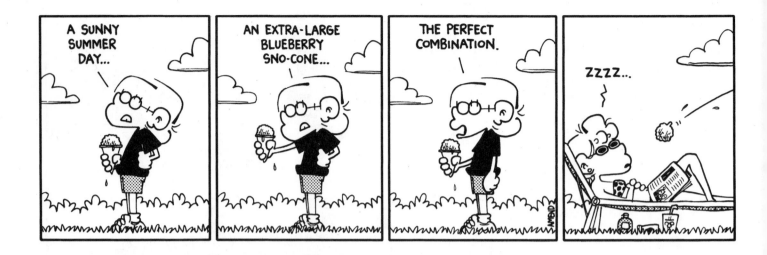

FoxTrot
BILL AMEND

36

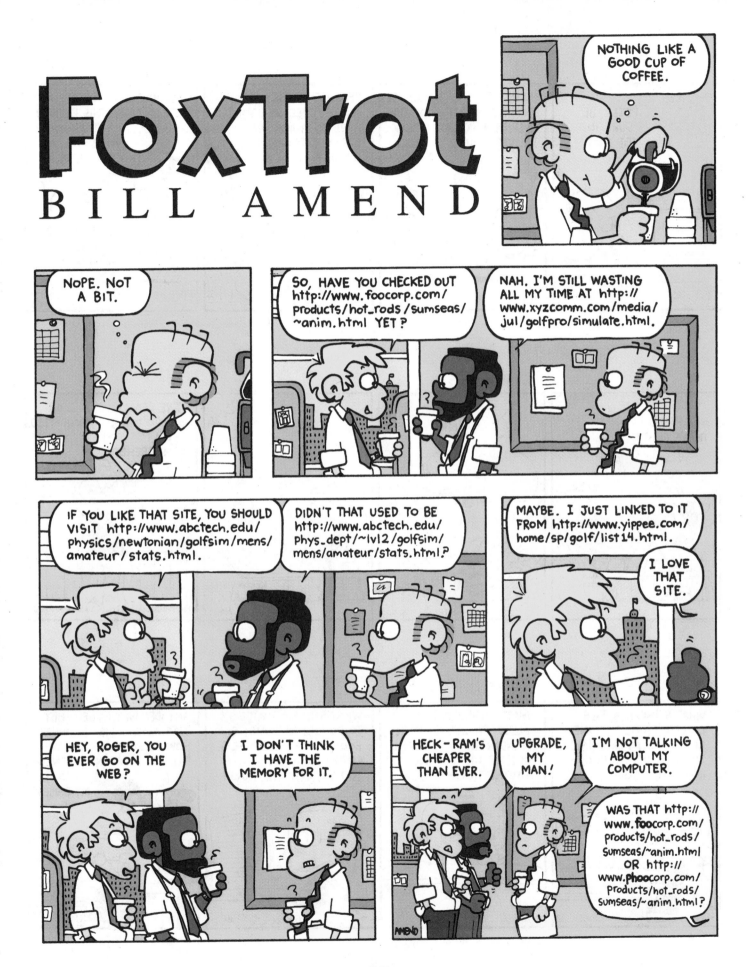

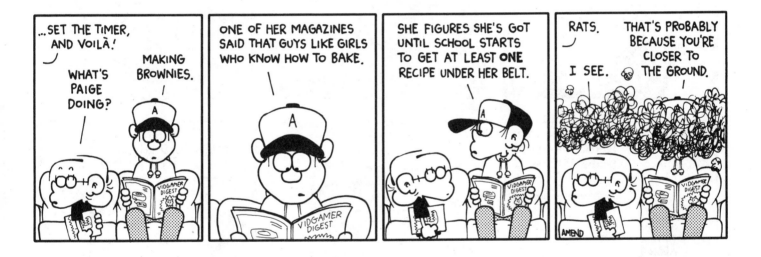

FoxTrot
BILL AMEND

40

FoxTrot
BILL AMEND

FoxTrot
BILL AMEND

I WONDER WHAT'S FOR DINNER.

I WONDER WHAT WAS FOR DINNER.

SEE THAT BRIGHT STAR DIRECTLY OVERHEAD, PETER?

THAT'S VEGA, THE HARP STAR. IT'S IN THE CONSTELLATION LYRA.

IT'S 27 LIGHT-YEARS AWAY.

THAT'S LIKE 159,000,000,000,000 MILES.

THAT'S SOME DISTANCE.

KINDA MAKES THE FOUR MILES I LED US DOWN THE WRONG TRAIL SEEM DOWNRIGHT INSIGNIFICANT, WOULDN'T YOU SAY?

IF WE DON'T FIND OUR CAMPSITE SOON, YOU'RE GOING TO BE SEEING A WHOLE LOT OF STARS, PAL.

AMEND

FoxTrot
BILL AMEND

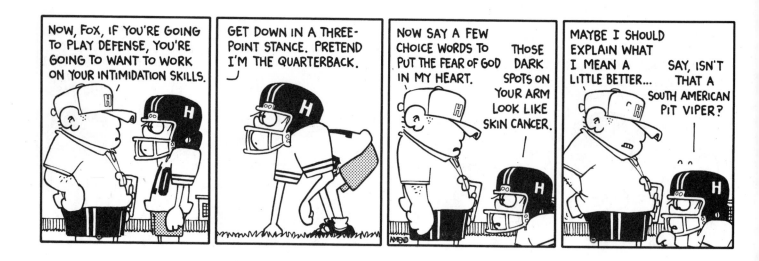

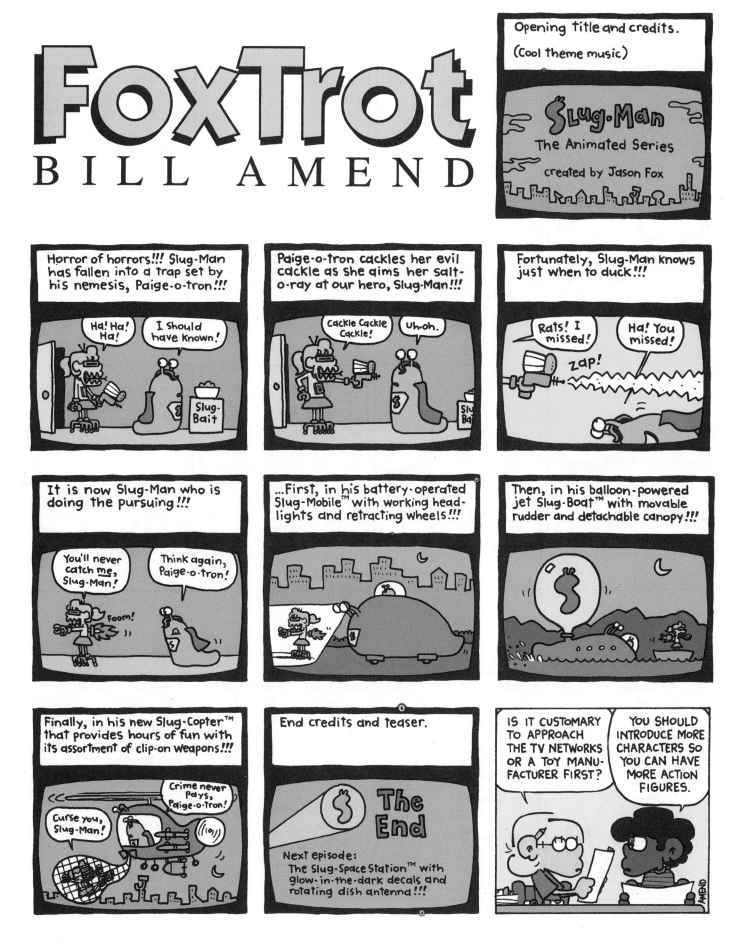

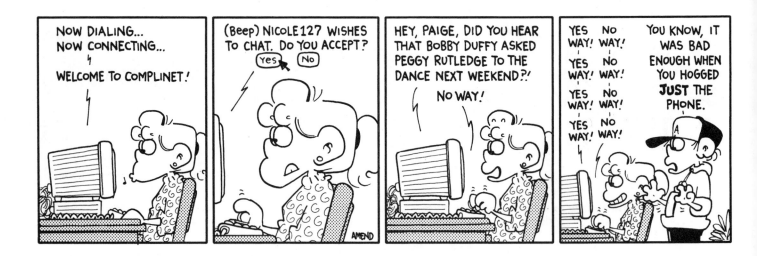

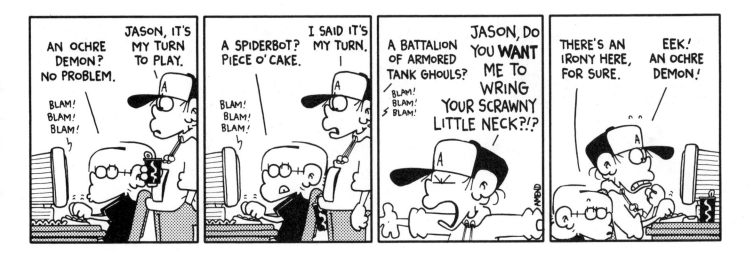

FoxTrot
BILL AMEND

Get out those scissors!

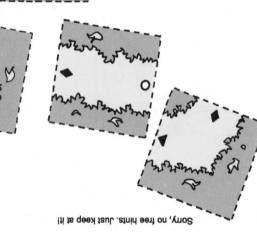

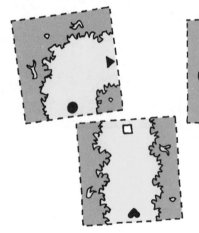

Sorry, no free hints. Just keep at it!

Jason's Challenge

Can you arrange these 12 pieces so that the dragon's fire forms one continuous loop?

Connect pieces by matching a white symbol to a black one of the same shape.

Right: Wrong: Wrong:

FoxTrot
BILL AMEND

FoxTrot
BILL AMEND

FoxTrot
BILL AMEND

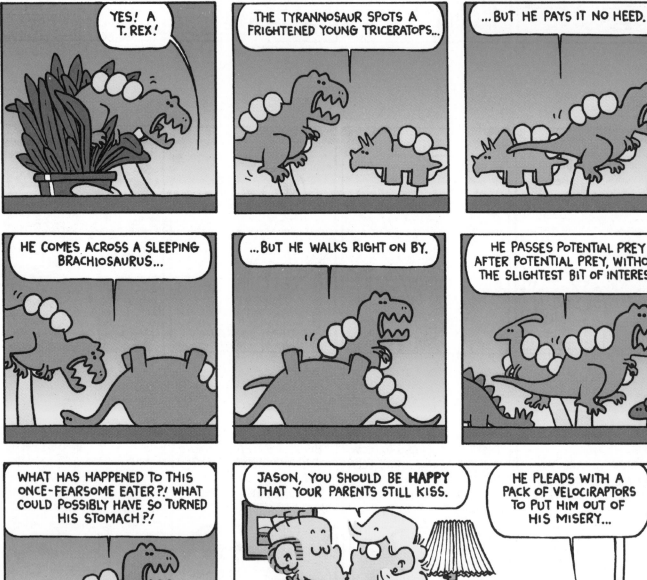

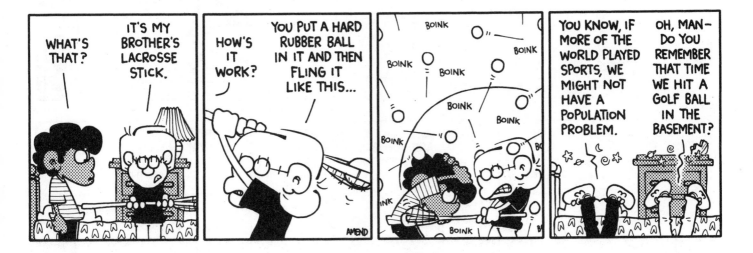

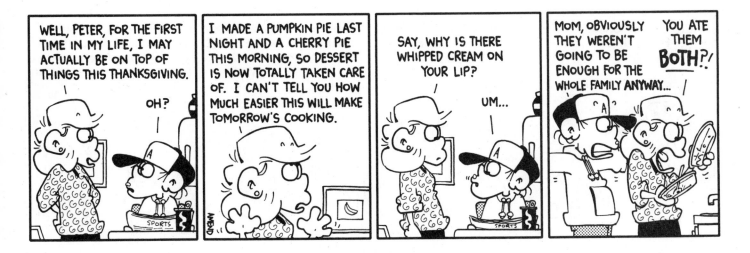

FoxTrot
BILL AMEND

93

99

FoxTrot
BILL AMEND

ALL I CAN SAY IS "MARMADUKE" HAD BETTER BE PRETTY BLEEPING FUNNY.

THANKS FOR GETTING US THIS CAMCORDER FOR CHRISTMAS, DAD!

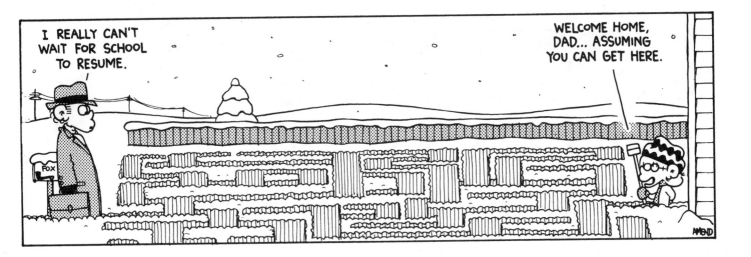

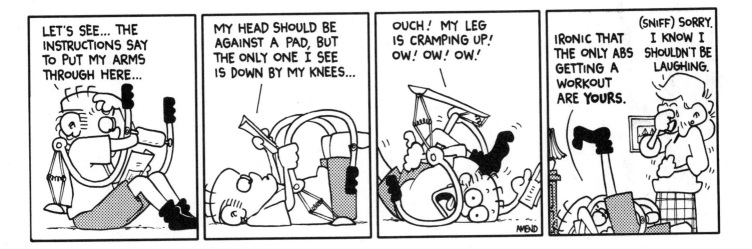

111

FoxTrot
BILL AMEND

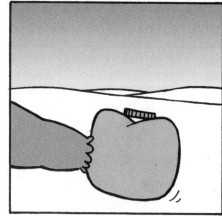

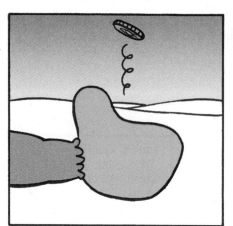

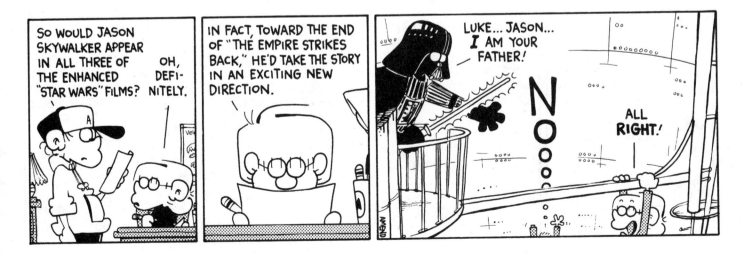

Panel 1: WAIT A MINUTE — YOU'D HAVE JASON SKYWALKER TURN TO THE DARK SIDE OF THE FORCE?! ... ABSOLUTELY. YOU BET.

Panel 2: I MEAN, THINK ABOUT IT. DARTH VADER WANTS SOMEONE TO HELP HIM RULE THE GALAXY. THE **GALAXY!** JASON CAN'T HELP IT IF HIS BROTHER LUKE'S A FOOL.

Panel 3: OBI-WAN HAS TAUGHT YOU WELL. ... I WILL NOT FIGHT YOU, FATHER. ... HE'S TALKING TO ME, YOU DOOFUS.

Panel 4: SO WHAT WOULD HAPPEN TO DARTH JASON AT THE END OF "RETURN OF THE JEDI"? ... HE'D SNEAK OFF THE NEW DEATH STAR JUST BEFORE THE REBELS BLOW IT UP.

Panel 5: THE CURRENT ENDING IS JUST TOO DARN HAPPY. **MY** VERSION WOULD LEAVE MOVIEGOERS CHILLED WITH THE KNOWLEDGE THAT THIS NEW ARCH-VILLAIN IS LURKING SOMEWHERE OUT THERE, READY TO RESURFACE WHEN THE SEQUELS EVENTUALLY GET MADE.

Panel 6: SO HOW WOULD HE ESCAPE? ... MY IDEA IS TO MAKE HIM A MASTER OF DISGUISE.

Panel 7: THEY **DID** IT, R2! ... LUCKY SHOT. I MEAN, BLEEP BLOOP.

Panel 8: PETER! PETER! I GOT A LETTER FROM LUCASFILM!

Panel 9: OPEN IT UP! WHAT'S IT SAY?! ... "DEAR MR. FOX: WE HAVE HAD A CHANCE TO REVIEW YOUR RECENT CORRESPONDENCE."

Panel 10: "UNFORTUNATELY, ALL WORK ON THE 'STAR WARS SPECIAL EDITION' TRILOGY WAS COMPLETED PRIOR TO RECEIPT OF YOUR LETTER AND WE THEREFORE HAVE NO CHOICE BUT TO PASS ON YOUR IDEAS." ... OH, WELL...

Panel 11: THAT'S NOT AN "UN" — IT'S A LITTLE BLOB OF TONER. ... AT LEAST THEY RETURNED MY DARTH JASON ACTION-FIGURE PROTOTYPE.

FoxTrot
BILL AMEND

FoxTrot
BILL AMEND

BBRRIINNGG!!!

OK, THERE'S THE BELL. YOU'RE ALL DISMISSED.

ALL BUT ONE, THAT IS.

class. I will not throw paper airplanes in class. I airplanes in class. I will not throw paper airplanes w paper airplanes in class. I will not throw paper ill not throw paper airplanes in class. I will not th class. I will not throw p airplanes in class. I v airplanes in class. I w

will not release insec rls' bathroom. I wi e insects into the om. I will not rele he girls' bathroom. elease insects into athroo

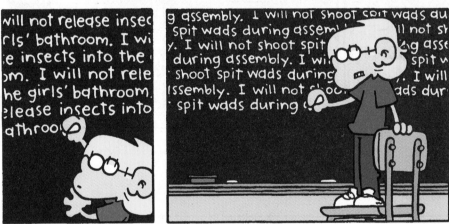

g assembly. I will not shoot spit wads du spit wads during assem y. I will not shoot spit during assembly. I wi shoot spit wads during ssembly. I will not sh spit wads during c ll not sh asse spit w . I will ads dur

elclup on my face. I will r ront of the school bus with ill not lie in front of the s with ketchup on my face. I e in front of the school bu ce. I will not lie in front us with ketchup on my fac fr

MISS O'MALLEY? FOR THE, UM, SLIDE PROJECTOR INCIDENT, WAS THAT 100 OR 200 TIMES?

500.

IS IT ME, OR HAS JASON'S PENMANSHIP GOTTEN REMARKABLY BETTER OF LATE?

THAT MEETING HIS TEACHER WANTS TO SCHEDULE MUST BE TO CONGRATULATE US.

FoxTrot
BILL AMEND

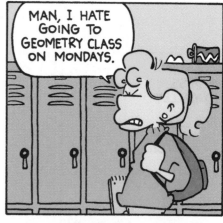

MAN, I HATE GOING TO GEOMETRY CLASS ON MONDAYS.

...AND TUESDAYS AND WEDNESDAYS AND THURSDAYS AND FRIDAYS.

AND IF **THESE** ANGLES ARE CONGRUENT, THEN WHAT?

THAT'S RIGHT. THESE SIDES MUST BE CONGRUENT AS WELL.

WHICH MEANS WE CAN SUBSTITUTE SEGMENT BC FOR AD BACK IN STEP THREE.

GIVING US...ANYONE? EXACTLY. ABCD IS, IN FACT, A RHOMBUS.

BUT THAT'S ONLY **PART** OF THE STORY HERE. BECAUSE, IF WE—...

POINK! POINK!

...UM, IF WE...

ZZZZ...

SOMEHOW, PAIGE, I DON'T THINK HE BOUGHT YOUR STORY THAT THESE PLASTIC GOLF BALL HALVES ARE PRESCRIPTION CONTACT LENSES.

AT LEAST HE GAVE THEM BACK. I'VE HEARD TALK WE'RE SEEING SLIDES IN FRENCH CLASS TODAY.

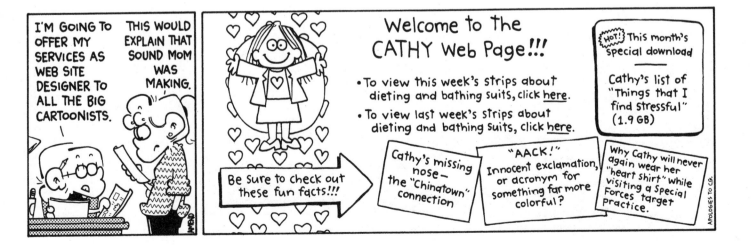

Panel 1 (left): SO, DO YOU THINK I SHOULD SEND MY WEB SITE IDEAS TO THE CARTOONISTS? OR TO THEIR SYNDICATES? CAN WE INCLUDE THE TRASH CAN AS OP- TION THREE?

Panel 2 (right):

Welcome to the DOONESBURY Web Page!!!

- To read today's strip, click here.
- To read the 22-page interview with German Finance Minister Theo Waigel from the November issue of The Economist, which helps put the punchline in some context, click here.

New! Download a listing of the entire cast of Doonesbury characters (not recommended for modems 28.8 kbps and slower)

AN IMPORTANT MESSAGE FROM UNCLE DUKE — Kids, I'm just Pretending to take all those drugs.

A Special Sneak-Peek at One of Next Week's Strips!!! — What is it, Al? Sir, the Ethiopian ambassador wants to know if it's all right to eat you. APOLOGIES TO GBT.

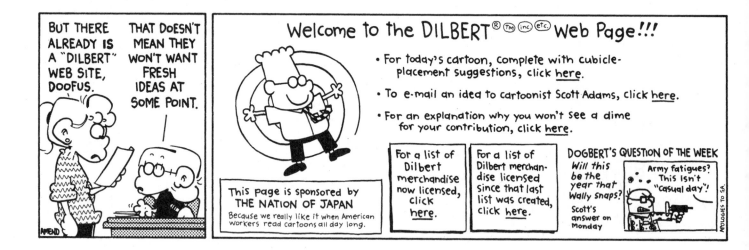

Panel 1 (left): BUT THERE ALREADY IS A "DILBERT" WEB SITE, DOOFUS. THAT DOESN'T MEAN THEY WON'T WANT FRESH IDEAS AT SOME POINT.

Panel 2 (right):

Welcome to the DILBERT ® ™ inc etc. Web Page!!!

- For today's cartoon, complete with cubicle-placement suggestions, click here.
- To e-mail an idea to cartoonist Scott Adams, click here.
- For an explanation why you won't see a dime for your contribution, click here.

This page is sponsored by THE NATION OF JAPAN
Because we really like it when American workers read cartoons all day long.

For a list of Dilbert merchandise now licensed, click here.

For a list of Dilbert merchandise licensed since that last list was created, click here.

DOGBERT'S QUESTION OF THE WEEK
Will this be the year that Wally snaps?
Scott's answer on Monday

Army fatigues? This isn't "casual day"! APOLOGIES TO SA.

Panel 1: I HEAR YOU'VE GIVEN UP TRYING TO DESIGN WEB SITES FOR CARTOONISTS. LET'S JUST SAY MY IDEAS WEREN'T GET- TING THE RECEPTION I EXPECTED.

Panel 2: OH? WHO'D YOU HEAR FROM? WELL, JIM DAVIS, WHO DOES "GARFIELD," SENT ME AN ENVELOPE FULL OF CONFETTI.

Panel 3: ...WHICH I INITIALLY TOOK AS A SIGN THAT HE WANTED ME TO CELEBRATE OUR NEW PARTNERSHIP.

Panel 4: UNTIL YOU NOTICED IT WAS MADE FROM THE LETTER YOU SENT HIM. THEN CHARLES SCHULZ SENT ME ASHES, WHICH I AT FIRST TOOK TO MEAN HE THOUGHT MY IDEAS WERE HOT...

FoxTrot
BILL AMEND

134

FoxTrot
BILL AMEND

DANG. I'VE BEEN SPOTTED.

NOT THAT I'M EXACTLY DRESSED FOR CAMOUFLAGE.

22...

23...

24!

I DID IT! I FOUND EVERY ONE OF THE HIDDEN EASTER EGGS!

PETER HAS ZERO! PAIGE HAS ZERO! I HAVE ALL 24! NOT ONLY IS THIS A VICTORY, BUT IT'S A COMPLETE AND TOTAL SHUTOUT!

EVERY YEAR THEY ALWAYS BEAT ME, BUT **THIS** YEAR THE TIDE HAS TURNED!

I AM THE NEW KING OF THE FOX FAMILY EASTER EGG HUNT! ALL HAIL ME!

I WISH THEY'D WAKE UP SO I CAN GLOAT.

SON, GO BACK TO BED — IT'S 6:15 A.M.

AMEND

141

143

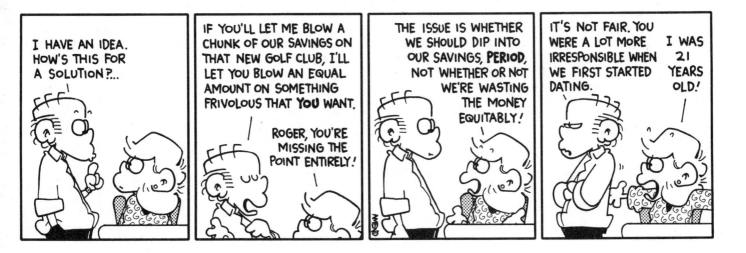

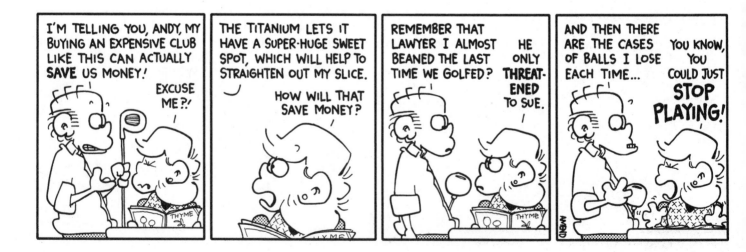

FoxTrot
BILL AMEND

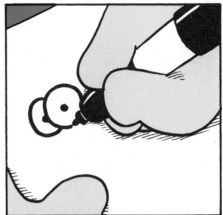

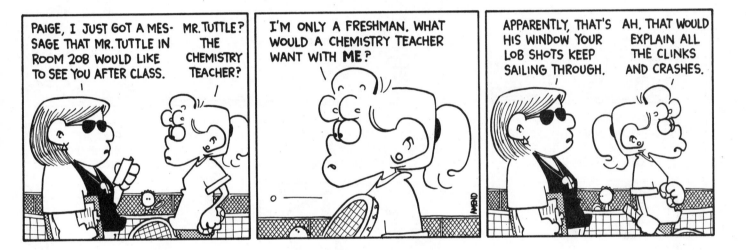

162

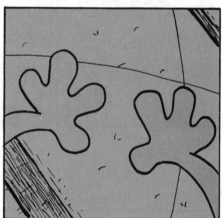

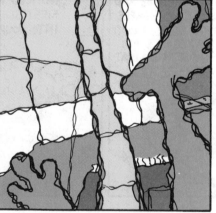

167

YOU KNOW, SWEETIE, MAYBE THIS SCIENCE CAMP WOULD BE GOOD FOR JASON.

HE'D BE WITH OTHER BRIGHT KIDS... SURROUNDED BY NATURE GETTING FRESH AIR... STUDYING SOMETHING HE LOVES...

BUT HE'S JUST SO YOUNG. BETTER TO SEND HIM OFF TO A CO-ED CAMP FOR THE SUMMER WHEN HE'S 10 THAN TO WAIT UNTIL HE'S, SAY, 13 OR 14.

JASON WITH HORMONES. NOW THERE'S A SCARY THOUGHT. I CAUGHT HIM DROOLING OVER PAIGE'S "COSMO" THE OTHER DAY, BUT APPARENTLY HE WAS JUST LOOKING AT A PENTIUM AD.

PETER! PETER! MOM AND DAD ARE LETTING ME GO TO SCIENCE CAMP THIS SUMMER!

COOL.

I MEAN, DID YOU CHECK OUT THIS BROCHURE?! IS THIS PLACE NOT PARADISE?!

WATERFALLS... HIKING TRAILS... CANOEING... A 3,000-YEAR-OLD REDWOOD GROVE... THIS DOES SOUND GREAT.

TREES, SCHMEES. GET TO THE PART ABOUT A T-1 LINE IN EVERY CABIN. "THINGS TO PACK: FLASHLIGHT, INSECT REPELLANT, MATHEMATICA 3.0."

HERE'S A LIST OF WAYS TO ENTERTAIN QUINCY WHILE I'M GONE.

HERE'S A LIST OF TV SHOWS I'D LIKE YOU TO TAPE WHILE I'M GONE.

AND HERE'S A LIST OF CANDIES AND COOKIES I LIKE, JUST IN CASE YOU WERE THINKING OF SENDING ME CARE PACKAGES. JASON, BY THE TIME I FINISH READING THESE, YOU'LL BE HOME FROM CAMP.

HMM. I SUPPOSE I COULD EDIT THOSE FIRST TWO LISTS DOWN SOME. HOW NICE OF YOU TO INCLUDE THESE AIR-FREIGHT PHONE NUMBERS.

173

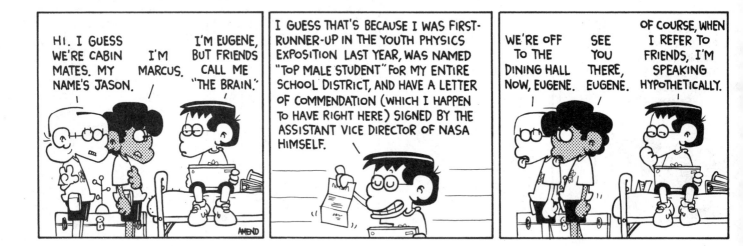

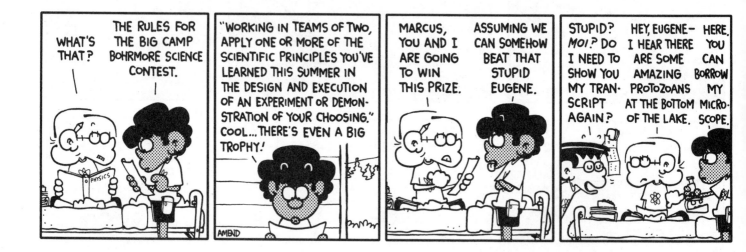

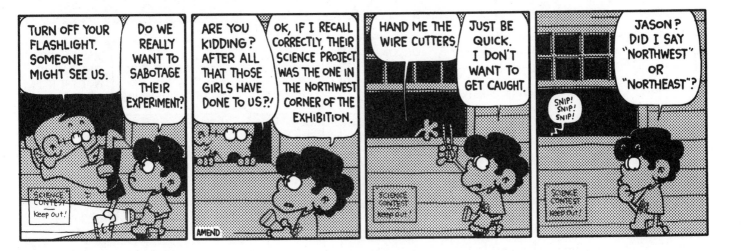

OK, THAT'S NINE VOTES FOR EUGENE AND MR. HAWKINS. NOW, HOW MANY OF YOU THINK THAT PHOEBE AND EILEEN HERE SHOULD WIN?

...5...6...7...8...

EIGHT VOTES... ANY MORE?... DID I GET EVERYONE?...

WELL, THEN, I GUESS WE HAVE OUR WIN— WAIT!

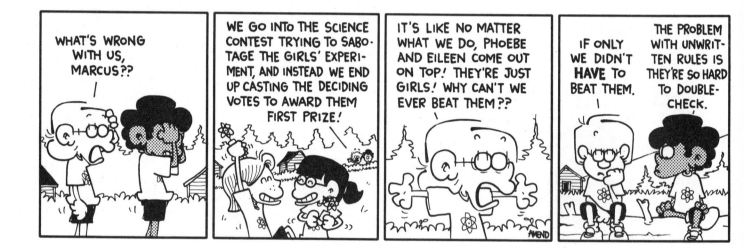

WHAT'S WRONG WITH US, MARCUS??

WE GO INTO THE SCIENCE CONTEST TRYING TO SABOTAGE THE GIRLS' EXPERIMENT, AND INSTEAD WE END UP CASTING THE DECIDING VOTES TO AWARD THEM FIRST PRIZE!

IT'S LIKE NO MATTER WHAT WE DO, PHOEBE AND EILEEN COME OUT ON TOP! THEY'RE JUST GIRLS! WHY CAN'T WE EVER BEAT THEM??

IF ONLY WE DIDN'T **HAVE** TO BEAT THEM.

THE PROBLEM WITH UNWRITTEN RULES IS THEY'RE SO HARD TO DOUBLE-CHECK.

WELL, GIRLS, IT'S YOUR LUCKY DAY.   BIG TIME.

No ood ights!

AFTER SOME DISCUSSION, MARCUS AND I HAVE DECIDED TO TAKE THE HIGH ROAD AND FORGIVE YOU FOR YOUR MANY DIABOLICAL ACTIONS AGAINST US THIS SUMMER. WE WILL NO LONGER SEEK REVENGE.

THE POISON IVY INCIDENT? FORGIVEN. THE PUDDING CUP INCIDENT? FORGIVEN. THE SNAILS IN OUR BEDSHEETS? ALL FORGIVEN.

BASICALLY, WHAT YOU'RE SAYING IS WE KICKED YOUR FANNIES.   BIG TIME.   THOSE ARE YOUR WORDS, NOT OURS.   UM, IF YOU WOULDN'T MIND SIGNING THIS DECLARATION OF TRUCE...

FoxTrot
BILL AMEND

AH, PARADISE.

MAKES ME ALMOST NOT MISS TELEVISION.

SO, WHERE TO NOW?

WELL, LET'S SEE...

WE COULD GO ACROSS THE LAKE AND SEE THAT BEAVER FAMILY AGAIN.

WE COULD GO BY THAT BIG ROCKY AREA AND LOOK FOR SNAKES SUNNING THEMSELVES.

WE COULD SWING PAST THAT INLET WHERE OUR COUNSELOR SAW THAT MOOSE.

OR WE COULD JUST PADDLE AROUND OVER BY THE DOCK.

WHAT KIND OF ANIMALS ARE OVER BY THE DOCK?

189

FoxTrot
BILL AMEND

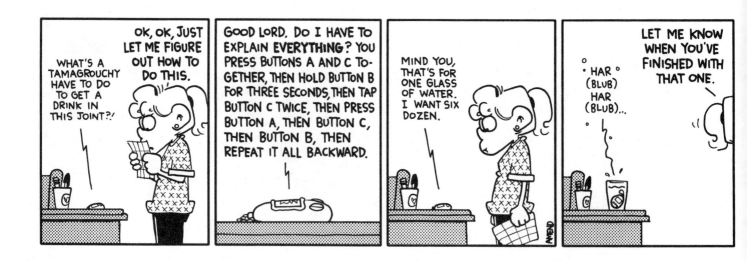

198

FoxTrot
BILL AMEND

PETER, I WANT YOU AND JASON TO GO BUY SCHOOL SUPPLIES TODAY.

I'M GIVING YOU EACH $20 TO SPEND. I TRUST YOU'RE MATURE ENOUGH TO HANDLE THIS MUCH MONEY.

ABSOLUTELY. OF COURSE. YOU BET.

SORRY. FEEL FREE TO CHIME IN. IT'S HARD TO TALK WITH MY MOUTH LIKE THIS. JASON, DON'T THINK I CAN'T HEAR THOSE CASH REGISTERS GOING OFF IN YOUR HEAD.

PETER, I'M TELLING YOU, ALL WE HAVE TO DO IS RECYCLE OUR NOTEBOOKS AND STUFF FROM LAST YEAR AND WE'LL HAVE $20 EACH TO SPEND ON SOMETHING **GOOD!**

I PROMISED MOM WE'D ONLY BUY SCHOOL SUPPLIES. PETER, PETER, PETER... DID MY ABSENCE ALL SUMMER UNDO ALL OF MY TEACHINGS?

ALLOW ME TO GIVE YOU A REFRESHER COURSE IN THE FINE ART OF RATIONALIZATION.

YOU KNOW, I BARELY GOT IN TROUBLE ALL SUMMER, EITHER. TAKE THIS WELL-LETTERED "PLASMA MAN" COMIC BOOK, AN EXCELLENT STUDY GUIDE FOR PENMANSHIP.

PETER, THINK ABOUT WHAT $20 CAN BUY!

ARMLOADS OF COMIC BOOKS! ENTIRE BOXES OF GUM! A 100 PERCENT COTTON "DUKE QUAKEM" T-SHIRT!

AND THAT'S JUST AT THE $20 LEVEL! IF WE **COMBINE** OUR SCHOOL SUPPLY MONEY, WE'LL HAVE A WHOPPING $40 TO SPEND! CAN YOU IMAGINE WHAT WE CAN GET WITH **THAT**?!

I'M HOPING WE CAN AFFORD A BRAIN SCAN FOR YOU. **TWO** "DUKE QUAKEM" T-SHIRTS! MY HEART SKIPPED A BEAT JUST SAYING THAT.

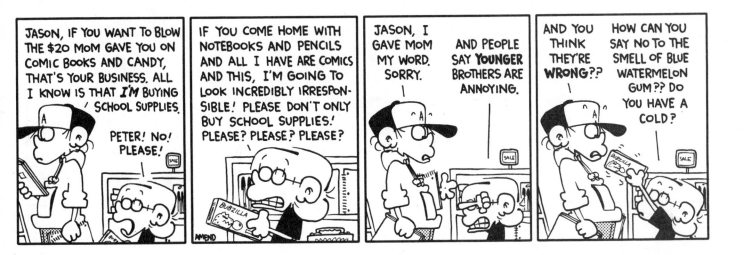

JASON, IF YOU WANT TO BLOW THE $20 MOM GAVE YOU ON COMIC BOOKS AND CANDY, THAT'S YOUR BUSINESS. ALL I KNOW IS THAT *I'M* BUYING SCHOOL SUPPLIES.

PETER! NO! PLEASE!

IF YOU COME HOME WITH NOTEBOOKS AND PENCILS AND ALL I HAVE ARE COMICS AND THIS, I'M GOING TO LOOK INCREDIBLY IRRESPONSIBLE! PLEASE DON'T ONLY BUY SCHOOL SUPPLIES! PLEASE? PLEASE? PLEASE?

JASON, I GAVE MOM MY WORD. SORRY.

AND PEOPLE SAY *YOUNGER* BROTHERS ARE ANNOYING.

AND YOU THINK THEY'RE *WRONG*??

HOW CAN YOU SAY NO TO THE SMELL OF BLUE WATERMELON GUM?? DO YOU HAVE A COLD?

YOU'RE REALLY BUYING SCHOOL SUPPLIES?

YUP.

AARGH! I CAN'T BELIEVE YOU'RE DOING THIS TO ME! THE BUYING SPREE OF A LIFETIME, THWARTED BY MY BOY SCOUT OF A BROTHER!

THE CHANCE TO BUY COMIC BOOKS... GUM BY THE BOX... THE NEW G.I. JIM NINJA STAR SET... ALL SQUANDERED BECAUSE *YOU* HAD TO PROMISE MOM WE WOULDN'T MISSPEND HER MONEY!

WAIT A MINUTE! YOUR SHOELACES WERE CROSSED! WE'VE GOT OURSELVES A LOOPHOLE!

GIVE IT UP, F.LEE. THE NOTEBOOKS ARE THATAWAY.

HOW WAS SHOPPING FOR SCHOOL SUPPLIES?

WELL, JASON WAS IN TYPICAL FORM.

I IMAGINE HE WANTED TO SPEND THE ENTIRE $20 I GAVE HIM ON COMIC BOOKS AND THE LIKE.

GEE, HOW'D YOU GUESS?

I TAKE IT HE EVENTUALLY CAME AROUND.

ONCE HE SAW THE AISLES OF "PLASMA MAN" NOTEBOOKS AND PENCILS.

IT KILLS ME TO SAY THIS, BUT THANK GOD FOR LICENSING.

PERSONALLY, I WENT WITH THE "BABE-WATCH" LINE OF PRODUCTS.

I FOUND A COUPLE DOLLARS IN MY DRESSER. CAN WE GO BACK FOR MORE?

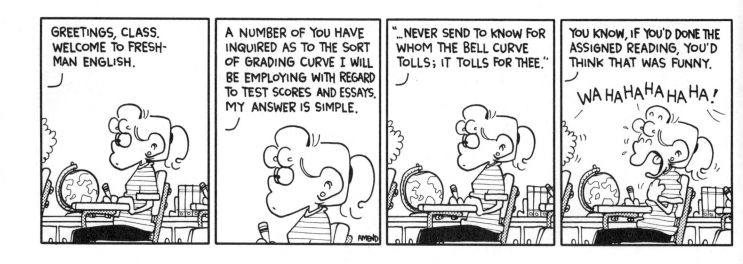

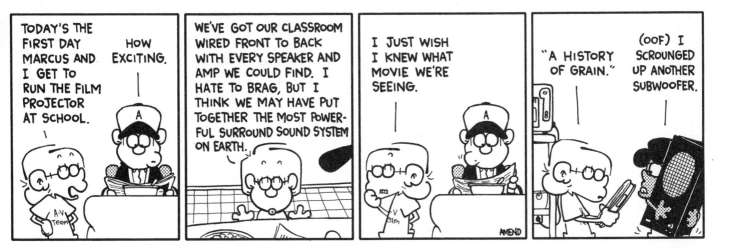

FoxTrot
BILL AMEND

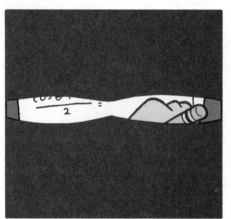

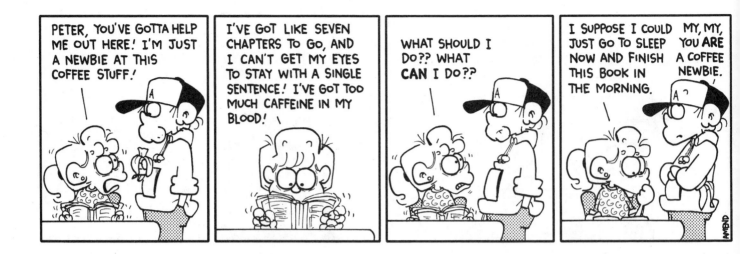

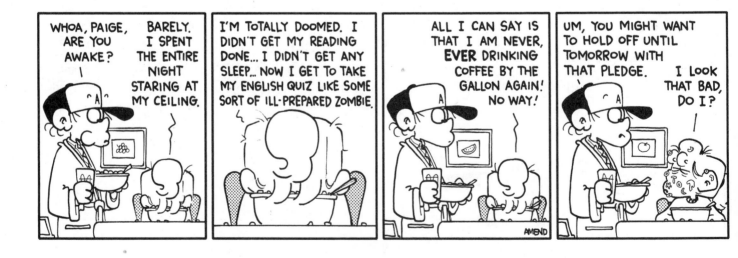

I KEEP FORGETTING TO TAKE MY GUM OUT BEFORE DINNER.

PETER, WHAT DO YOU WANT FOR LUNCH TODAY?

OH, GOSH, I DUNNO...

PEANUT BUTTER AND JELLY WOULD BE GOOD... BOLOGNA AND CHEESE WOULD BE GOOD... TURKEY... TUNA... HAM... SALAMI... THAT EGG SALAD YOU SOMETIMES MAKE...

SO, ANY OF THOSE?

NO, NO– ALL OF THOSE.

DID I MENTION I SAW OUR GROCER TEST-DRIVING A PORSCHE LAST WEEK?

YOU KNOW, THESE "FAMILY-SIZED" BOXES ARE GROSSLY MISLABELED.

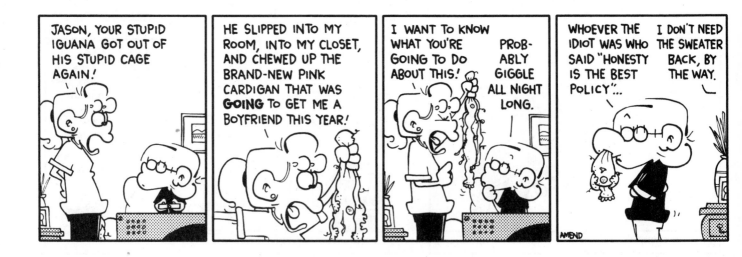

JASON, YOUR STUPID IGUANA GOT OUT OF HIS STUPID CAGE AGAIN!

HE SLIPPED INTO MY ROOM, INTO MY CLOSET, AND CHEWED UP THE BRAND-NEW PINK CARDIGAN THAT WAS **GOING** TO GET ME A BOYFRIEND THIS YEAR!

I WANT TO KNOW WHAT YOU'RE GOING TO DO ABOUT THIS!

PROB-ABLY GIGGLE ALL NIGHT LONG.

WHOEVER THE IDIOT WAS WHO SAID "HONESTY IS THE BEST POLICY"...

I DON'T NEED THE SWEATER BACK, BY THE WAY.

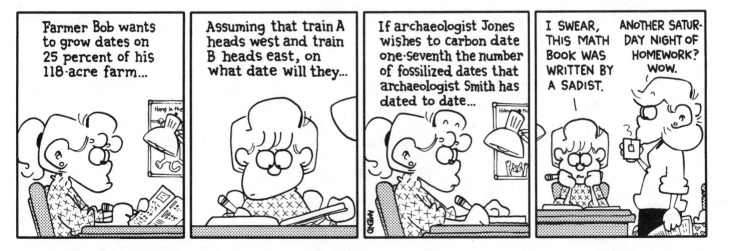

FoxTrot
BILL AMEND

FoxTrot

BILL AMEND

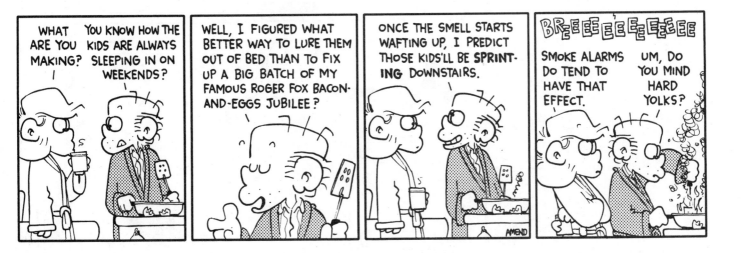

Panel 1: HI, SWEETIE. HOW'S THE CONVENTION GOING?

Panel 2: OH, WE'VE BEEN MANAGING JUST FINE. WHAT CAN GO WRONG IN FOUR DAYS, RIGHT?

Panel 3: NOW, THEN, ABOUT YOUR FLIGHT BACK TOMORROW... YOU GET IN WHEN - 7 P.M.? 8 P.M.?... OH, 4 P.M.... THAT EARLY...

Panel 4: "STRESS"? NO, NO - THAT'S EXCITEMENT YOU DETECT IN MY VOICE. I SWEAR, DAD. EVEN *I* KNOW HOW TO RUN THE DISHWASHER CORRECTLY.

Panel 5: KIDS, I JUST GOT OFF THE PHONE WITH YOUR MOTHER. SHE'S PLANNING TO BE HOME SOMETIME AROUND 5 P.M. TOMORROW.

Panel 6: THAT GIVES US LESS THAN 24 HOURS TO CLEAN UP THIS LITTLE FLOOD WE'VE CREATED. *WE'VE* CREATED??

Panel 7: LOOK, LET'S NOT WORRY ABOUT WHO'S TO BLAME AT THIS POINT. I'LL ADMIT I'M TO BLAME FOR ALL THE WATER SNAKES. WATER SNAKES?!

Panel 8: JASON, YOU'RE NOT HELPING. ...THE FOUR-FOOTERS, AT LEAST. AAAA! (SPLASH! SPLASH! SPLASH!)

Panel 9: PETER, TRY OPENING THE BACK DOOR. MAYBE WE CAN DRAIN THE WATER THAT WAY.

Panel 10: YES! YES! IT'S WORKING! YOUR MOTHER **ISN'T** GOING TO RETURN TO FIND HER HOUSE IS ONE BIG LAKE!

Panel 11: (no dialogue)

Panel 12: UM, WHICH IS WORSE - A LAKE OR A SWAMP? WANT ME TO TURN THE WATER BACK ON?

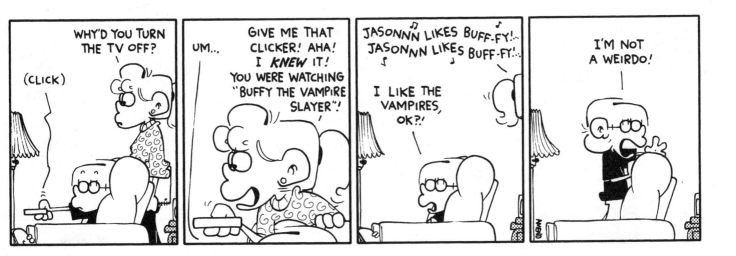

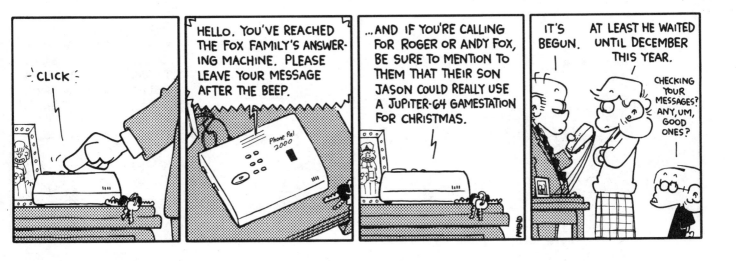

242

FoxTrot
BILL AMEND

AAAA! PETER! PETER! AAAA! PETER! PETER!

WHAT?

AAAA! IN THE GARAGE! AAAA! IN THE GARAGE!

WHAT ABOUT THE GARAGE?

AAAA! I SAW... AAAA! I SAW...

YOU SAW WHAT??

AAAA! IT'S LIKE A DREAM! AAAA! IT'S LIKE A DREAM!

JASON, WILL YOU CALM DOWN AND TELL ME WHAT'S GOING ON?!

AMEND

(Gasp Gasp) IN THE CORNER (Gasp Gasp) OF THE GARAGE (Gasp Gasp) IS AN OBVIOUS PRESENT FOR US THAT HASN'T YET BEEN WRAPPED!

IS IT SOMETHING GOOD? WHAT IS IT?

OH, BY THE WAY, FRED ASKED ME TO HOLD ONTO SOME FANCY COMPUTER HE GOT FOR HIS KIDS. HE DOESN'T WANT THEM STUMBLING UPON IT BEFORE CHRISTMAS.

WHAT ON **EARTH** ARE THOSE TWO BOYS SQUEALING ABOUT??

Comics 101

One of the things I've noticed in my conversations with people over the ten-plus years I've been creating *FoxTrot* is that a lot of you really like to read comic strips. Sometimes mine, even. That's good. Keep it up. Buy those books. But I've also noticed that not many of you seem to know a whole lot about how comic strips are created and by what process they get into and stay in your newspapers. Despite the ubiquitousness of the works, the *work* of cartooning is apparently downright obscure. And that's not so good.

For starters, it means I have to answer the same bajillion questions over and over again each time I run into one of you at the bait shop. "Where do you get your ideas?" "How far in advance do you work?" "Hee hee—think Quincy'd like these here night crawlers?" But it also means one of the more communicative occupations in our culture perhaps hasn't been doing enough communicating about itself, and the more this continues, the more the art of cartooning risks slowly wilting in the darkness. After all, people tend not to do things they know nothing about (home repair projects excluded). Imagine the next Charles Schulz or Lynn Johnston being out there and never putting together a comic strip submission to send off in the hopes of getting a syndication deal, not because he or she couldn't, but because he or she had no idea he or she *could*. Likewise, imagine readers never expressing displeasure to their newspapers about mediocre comics or microscopic printing, again, not because they can't, but because they had no idea they *should*.

But there is always hope. Being the conscientious fellow I am, and because my publisher tells me I have six blank pages to fill in this book, I will now explain to you in meticulous and overtly biased generalities the heretofore mysterious art and business of comic strip cartooning. And if the three of you reading this go out and tell the six billion other inhabitants of the earth, we might actually do some good.

How Comics Are Created

Not equally, that's for sure. I don't mean that as a catty comment about the quality of some works, although I have been known to lie. What I mean is that every cartoonist I know seems to work differently. There aren't any hard-and-fast rules to writing and drawing a comic strip, which is for me part of the creative appeal. What ultimately matters is what you end up with, not necessarily how it is you did it. Bill Watterson once told me how he inked part of a *Calvin and Hobbes* strip with a stick from his yard in order to achieve a certain look. Tell me that's not pretty cool.

Something I've always found puzzling is how often the television industry tries to base a sitcom series or episode around the wacky life of a syndicated cartoonist. Maybe I'm unique among my peers, but my workday surely must rank somewhere behind tax preparation as far as interesting theater goes. I work alone, at home, in a room above my garage. I read E-mail and snail mail, make phone calls, and of course, write and draw cartoons, typically into the night. Maybe once every three months someone will invite me to lunch, but more often than not I eat peanut butter and jelly or swing by a fast-food joint. And then I do it all again the next day. My point being, it's not a job chock-full of Hollywood-style glamour and excitement. It's more often than not stressful, cerebral, solitary work.

But there are a lot of upsides, the biggest and most obvious is that I get to spend most of every day creating a comic strip that millions of people seem to enjoy. Also, I don't have to shave and can dress as I please, which is awfully nice, except for those times when the doorbell rings. And I can play my stereo really loudly or watch TV while I'm drawing (not without risks, however—more than one cartoon has been messed up because of a particularly funny Letterman quip sending my hand bouncing during inking). And I can go tickle my kids whenever the urge strikes. And I don't have a boss that's going to yell at me if I, say, choose to play Quake on my computer when I should be writing this essay. It's a lot like being in college, but with money.

But, as I said, we in this field are all different. Some syndicated cartoonists also have "day" jobs. Some have outside studios. Some have writing partners or art assistants or sixty-employee corporations. It's all a matter of personal preference (and what you can afford). What's nice about cartooning is that you don't *need* the big support staffs and offices and collaborators to produce the best work. At least, that's what I tell myself as I toil on by my lonesome.

The number one question that I am asked by people upon hearing what I do is "Where do you get your ideas?" Sometimes it's even meant as a compliment. The truth is, I don't really know. Usually my strip ideas come from thinking really, really hard in a sort of "what if . . . ?" way. I take a subject or opening setup and start conversations between the characters going in my head, and when one seems to lead somewhere funny or interesting, I quickly write it down and work on the best way to stage and word things. Often nothing works and I move on to a new subject or angle. Once in a rare while an entire strip idea will pop into my head in usable form, but not as often as I'd like. One thing I find helpful is to try to do all of my writing one day each week. This removes the pressure of having to be funny every day. Once the strips are written, I can spend the rest of the week drawing them, funny mood or not.

The second most common question I hear is "How far in advance do you work?" Typically on TV shows, the syndicated cartoonist is drawing tomorrow's comic today. Much to my syndicate's relief, I'm not quite that timely with my work. In fact, no comic strip cartoonist is to my knowledge. Because most papers still prefer the delivery of their comics on paper via mail, cartoonists need to get their work in well ahead of the release date to allow for distribution. I turn in each week of *FoxTrot* dailies about two weeks prior to release. Because Sunday strips require coloring and often separate printing schedules, I turn those in some six weeks in advance. Most of my peers in this business strike me as mildly more responsible types, and I'm guessing the majority of cartoonists turn their strips in a month or more in advance.

So, it's two weeks before release, I've written my week of strips, now what do I do? Oh, this little, teeny tiny task of drawing and inking them. I think I'm somewhat unique in this field in that I find the drawing of my strip a lot more challenging than the writing of it. I don't have a formal background in art (in case that wasn't obvious) and even though my drawing style appears simple, it still takes me lots and lots of erasing and redrawing before I have cartoons I'm ready to ink. Many cartoonists, especially in the comic book trade, employ brushes or crow-quill pens dipped in ink for this, often imbuing the work with beautiful suggestions of depth and weight and mood. Being, as I am, chronically pressed for time, I have chosen the simpler method of tracing my pencil lines with a permanent black marker. Once my dailies are inked, I add self-adhesive shading film to give that dotted look to certain items. Then it's all off to my syndicate for editing and distribution.

My Sunday strips, requiring the addition of color, are accompanied by a hand-colored photocopy in which I identify the colors I want using numbers from a standardized chart of 124 color choices. This is all sent to a company that specializes in electronically adding color to comics via computer.

Ah, what about computers, you ask? Well, if you didn't ask, you should have, because it's a good question. As with most other modes of graphic art, computers are playing a larger and larger role in the production of comics. While I prefer at this point to render my strips by hand with pencils and pens on paper, a growing number of comic strips are being put together digitally. A cartoonist's handwriting can be converted to a font, line art can be scanned or drawn directly on screen and manipulated once there, and the addition of grays and colors via one's computer allows for a host of interesting gradations and effects. I think computers and software still have a way to go before they can match the flexibility and ease of use of pens and pencils, but there's no doubt in my mind that computers will be shaping the look of our comic art—in some good ways and some bad ways—more and more in the near future.

The Business of Comic Strips

Most every comic strip you see in a newspaper anymore is distributed by a handful of companies called syndicates (don't let the word fool you—they're much scarier than they sound). This means that before a cartoonist can seriously hope to see his or her comic strip in a newspaper, he or she must first land a deal with one of these syndicates, which is no easy task. Thousands and thousands of comic strip submissions from aspiring professional and amateur cartoonists arrive in syndicate offices by mail over the course of each year, from which each syndicate chooses at most two or three to distribute. It took me nearly three years of submitting and resubmitting various batches of FoxTrot—as an unpublished amateur straight out of college—before Universal Press Syndicate offered me a contract in 1987.

How do syndicates choose the select few strips they do? Not without a little finger crossing, I can tell you that. Even once syndicated, there's a high likelihood of failure for a strip. I'm told that close to half of all new comic strips sold to papers wither and die within two years. What syndicates try to do is sign up a limited number of new strips each year that they believe they can effectively sell to a large number of newspapers. Note that I did not say they necessarily select the most innovative or best drawn or funniest strips. Sometimes this is the same as being marketable to papers, sometimes it isn't.

And how are these strips marketed? In my syndicate's case there are about half a dozen salespeople who drive all around the United States and Canada pitching strips in person to the various newspapers' editors. It's not very efficient and rather costly, especially when you consider the average paper pays maybe ten dollars a week for a strip (twenty dollars if they buy the Sunday version too). This is one reason why most syndicates ask that cartoonists sign long-term contracts. Back at the syndicate, there are probably a dozen support people assisting the process in various ways and working with papers after the sale. For international sales, responsibilities are split between syndicate personnel and overseas agents with third parties preparing translated versions of the comics.

Syndicates do a great many things behind the scenes for a cartoonist, not the least of which is to act as editor for the work. Besides correcting the too-frequent spelling blunders and grammatical car wrecks in *FoxTrot,* my syndicate editor for the past ten years has been a wonderful sounding board for almost every one of my stabs at humor before I would commit the idea to ink on paper. I think most successful cartoonists have a pretty good sense for what is or isn't funny, but a trusted second opinion doesn't hurt.

While I have virtually unlimited freedom to write about what interests me, I don't have total freedom under my syndication agreement, and it's my editor's job to reign me in if I step out of bounds and write something that's going to get me canceled by every paper I'm in. My syndicate has, to their credit, never told or suggested to me what to write, but they have on a few occasions told me what not to write. And in retrospect, I'm usually glad they did.

Having never been a newspaper comics editor myself, I only have a few gray hairs. I also can't say for certain what attracts them to some comics over others, except that I do know human nature, and it's normal human nature to not want to have to explain to your boss why the newspaper's phone lines are jammed with calls from foaming-at-the-mouth fans of the comic you just axed. And believe me, just about any strip that's been around a while has a battalion of these fans just ready to spring into action. So, as you may have noticed, changes on the comics page aren't exactly a weekly occurrence at most papers, and my hunch is the sorts of strips that do get the privilege of being added most often come with a host of ready-made demographic or sales justifications for both boss and irate subscriber attached. In other words, quirky, personal strips have it tougher than big-name strips or strips about safe, salable topics. I could be wrong, but my experience reading America's funny pages suggests otherwise.

Speaking of "safe" strips, it's worth pointing out one of the dilemmas newspapers face with comics. Unlike television, where people can choose specific shows like items on a menu, the comics page is more like a big, open buffet. Strips with mature themes may be seen by children. Strips with juvenile themes may be seen by adults. While I think there is a huge hunger on the part of many comics readers for edgier fare than what is currently so prevalent, it's worth understanding that editors have a broad demographic of reader sensitivities to consider, and I for one don't entirely blame them for a somewhat conservative approach. That said, I do have concerns that if comics pages are too soft and safe, there is the risk of eventually driving both readers and artists to the point of indifference toward this art form.

When a newspaper buys a strip, typically it gets territorial exclusivity to that strip. This is why in two-newspaper towns, you rarely see a strip that appears in both papers. It's a practice that makes sense from the newspapers' point of view, but it has some real downsides for the cartoonist. For starters, there's usually no expiration or renewal of the exclusivity so long as the paper buys the strip, which means there will almost never be any sort of bidding wars or contention among papers for popular comics. Also, some editors will buy a strip and then not run it, knowing this will keep it blocked from the competition in case it turns out to be a hit.

As I mentioned, newspapers pay something close to ten dollars a week on average for a daily comic strip. Big papers in competitive markets may pay many hundreds per week, but the average rate is pretty modest. The agreement most cartoonists have with their syndicates calls for a fifty-fifty split of net revenues, which means the name of the game is to be in as many papers as possible, especially early on when a cartoonist may be struggling to make even minimum wage. The syndicates want sales, the cartoonists want sales, and the newspapers have less and less space they're willing to give.

Which has meant that the gradual shrinking of comics by space-conscious newspapers has been met with limp resistance by many of us in the field. We're too hungry for sales to tell the newspapers to print fewer strips if space is at such a premium. And it's not without effect. The shrinking of comics by newspapers over the last few decades has absolutely had an impact on the styles of art and writing that are so prevalent on the funny pages today. Less space means fewer panels, fewer words, simpler art, and simpler staging (I rarely do daily strips with three characters interacting, for example, because of space constraints). There are, thank goodness, wonderful exceptions, but I think the general trend is unquestionable and unfortunate.

Similar to the shrinking of comics, but worse, is the practice by some newspapers to distort strips with computers or lenses to effectively squash the panels to make them smaller along the vertical axis. This allows them to squeeze more strips onto a page top to bottom, but it also ruins the look of the artwork. Circles become ovals and characters become stocky and short. Again, cartoonists and syndicates should complain, but too often we don't because of fear of losing a client.

A growing outlet for comics these days is the Internet, which I believe is going to be the greatest boon for comic strip fans and creators since the invention of the refrigerator magnet. My syndicate currently sells my same-day strip to a number of newspaper Web sites, week-old strips to non-newspaper Web sites, and posts two-week old strips and a whole host of other material on the *FoxTrot* Web site. The potential to reach millions of comics fans who might not see my work in their local paper (or who may not even read their local paper) is really quite exciting. My hunch is the Internet is going to pump a lot of fresh energy and life into this business, and I look forward to seeing what happens, both as a comic strip creator and reader.

Finally, I'd be remiss if I didn't mention that to supplement the income from newspapers, many cartoonists (including yours truly) earn royalties from the sale of books and calendars and whatever else they might get acceptable offers to do. Some cartoonists pursue these licensing opportunities with great zeal, some recoil from the notion entirely. As with the methods of creating a strip, the way a strip and its characters are used commercially varies a good deal among the members of this profession, and I think it's best to respect each artist's wishes for his or her creation. Or at least pretend like we do when writing essays.

So, That's It

The comic strip art and business in a nutshell. Okay, a long nutshell. As I mentioned back in my introduction, part of my motivation for writing this was to educate the potential cartoonist about some of the realities of this profession, good and bad. Eleven years ago I was a twenty-four-year-old unemployed physics major nobody living with my parents sending comic strip submissions off in the mail. Now I'm writing about it in the back of my strip's eighteenth book collection. I am living proof that this amazing job is open to anybody with the right mixture of luck and talent, but only if you know to try.

As for fans of comics, I hope that my explaining some of the behind-the-scenes workings and politics of this business will serve as a clue that many of the things you might want to see improved on the comics page are not etched in stone, but are often the result of newspapers and syndicates and, yes, cartoonists looking after their own self-interests. What needs to happen is for readers to look after their own interests as well. When you like a strip, tell the paper. When you don't, tell the paper. If your newspaper treats its strips in a way you don't approve of, perhaps by shrinking or squishing or colorizing them, don't just grumble to yourself, grumble to the paper. If you have suggestions, let them be heard. Ultimately, all of us in this business work for you, the readers, and you really can affect what you see in print. Again, only if you know to try.

Thanks for your time and interest. I hope this has been and will be helpful. Camp dismissed.

Bill Amend
July 1998